Original title:
The Secret Shore

Copyright © 2025 Creative Arts Management OÜ
All rights reserved.

Author: Sebastian Whitmore
ISBN HARDBACK: 978-1-80581-477-1
ISBN PAPERBACK: 978-1-80581-004-9
ISBN EBOOK: 978-1-80581-477-1

Shores Unspoken, Stories Untold

Beneath the waves where secrets play,
Crabs wear hats and dance all day.
Seashells gossip, oh what a chat,
Fish in tuxedos, imagine that!

The sun's a chef with a brow so proud,
Flipping pancakes for the crowd.
Seagulls swoop, but they are fakes,
Miming dives for crumbs and flakes.

Turtles tell tales with a wink and a nod,
Of beach ball wars; it gets quite odd.
Dolphins giggle, ride the swell,
Playing tag with a starfish, oh what the shell!

On sandy paths where lizards prance,
They throw a party, so take a chance!
Join the fun, but mind your hat,
For playful waves will steal it, just like that!

The Cove of Untold Stories

In the cove where fish tell tales,
The seaweed dances, and laughter sails.
Clams wear hats, and shells flip-flop,
Even the crabs have a comic shop.

Pirates spill secrets in rhyming disguise,
While jellyfish giggle, oh what a surprise!
Turtles hold parties, with snacks so sweet,
Stop by for a joke, it's quite the treat!

Moonlit Footprints on the Beach

Under the moon, footprints abound,
Oh look, a raccoon has come to hound!
Sandcastles threaten to tumble and fall,
As starfish prank say, 'We're here for the ball!'

Seagulls debate over who stole the fries,
While crabs do the cha-cha with sneaky lies.
The night dances lightly with whimsical glee,
Come join the fun, you'll want to be free!

Secrets Beneath the Surface

Beneath the waves, fish gossip away,
Trading their secrets, come join their play!
Octopuses giggle, with ink they confide,
In a party of chaos, the sea is their guide.

Mermaids swap rumors, they've got the scoop,
While turtles just nod, snagging snacks from a stoop.
Bubbles bring laughter, like jokes from a jar,
Dive in for the fun, it's never bizarre!

The Lure of Distant Shores

Shores far away call with a wink,
Where lost socks dance and mermaids drink!
Here's a treasure map, but who will confess,
That X marks the spot where we find the mess?

Seashells trade secrets of lands they've seen,
While surfboards gossip of waves that are mean.
In the distance, a whale sings a tune,
Join the hilarity beneath the bright moon!

Fables Carried by the Wind

There once was a crab in a tiny shell,
He danced on the sand, oh so swell.
He called to the gull, with a wink and a grin,
"Join me for laughter, let the games begin!"

A fish in a hat sang a catchy tune,
The starfish giggled, 'It's quite the afternoon!'
With bubbles and giggles, the tide rolled about,
Splashing their secrets, laughing out loud.

Beyond the Horizon's Gaze

A turtle wore goggles, dreaming of flight,
He soared with the seagulls, feeling so light.
But alas, the tide pulled him back to the ground,
He chuckled, 'At least I'm the fastest around!'

Through waves they would tumble, a merry parade,
With fishy confetti, their joy never fade.
They tasted the salty fun in the breeze,
Next stop: a party beneath the palm trees!

The Enchanted Cove of Dreams

A dolphin named Dot loved to play pranks,
She'd tickle the whales; they gave her their thanks.
With a flip and a splash, she'd vanish from sight,
Returning with seaweed, a wig of delight!

A crab with a trumpet joined in her spree,
He puffed out his belly, playing loud and free.
The sun dipped below, painting skies of delight,
While laughter and silliness danced through the night.

Nightfall Over Silent Waters

A clam told a story that made fish all laugh,
About a wise octopus who took a hot bath.
With bubbles and bubbles that caused quite a scene,
He slipped and he flipped, oh what a routine!

Beneath the stars, with laughter so bright,
They played peek-a-boo with the glow of the night.
From waves crashing softly to dreams that ignite,
Their giggles rang out, a joyous delight!

In the Quiet of Coastal Twilight

Seagulls plotting with their caw,
Making jokes about the law.
The crabs all dance in tiny shoes,
As fishermen share tall tales of blues.

Sandy toes and sunburned backs,
Ice cream cones, the perfect snacks.
A sunset hue spills like jam,
While starfish giggle, 'Oh, what a sham!'

The Starlit Path to Hidden Waters

Under the moon, the tides will play,
While fish serenade, in their own way.
A starfish said, 'Behold my strength!'
As he flexed in the sand at arm's length.

A dolphin dove to steal the show,
With flips and tricks, an underwater pro.
Crabs watched with popcorn in their claws,
The ocean's spectacle earns applause!

Driftwood Tales from an Unknown Land

Driftwood whispers secrets grand,
Of pirate treasure, lost in the sand.
A wise old log with tales to tell,
Mumbles, 'All treasure goes well with gel!'

The shells all chuckle as they align,
'We're not just pretty, but also divine.'
Octopi scribble with a felt-tip pen,
Stories of mishaps from way back when.

Beneath the Surface of the Sea

Down below, it's quite a spree,
Where fish throw parties, wild and free.
A clownfish jokes, 'I'm never blue!'
'Just reef-tastic, how about you?'

Anemones dance like they're in a ball,
With jellyfish spinning, having a ball.
Octopuses juggle, 'Look at me go!'
'We're just a little wet, don't steal the show!'

Enchanted Driftwood and Forgotten Dreams

On the beach where flip-flops roam,
A crab wore shades, claiming a home.
Driftwood danced, a waltz with glee,
While seagulls debated, 'What's for tea?'

A starfish giggled, 'Look at me!'
It tried to high-five a nearby tree.
Shells whispered secrets, oh so grand,
About mermaids lost, with seashell bands.

The ocean sang a bubbly tune,
As dolphins joined beneath the moon.
With waves that tickled sandy toes,
And laughter chased where sea breeze blows.

So if you wander to that place,
Prepare for fun and plenty of grace.
For on this shore, both wild and weird,
Surprises pop up, never feared.

Shadows Beneath the Crescent Moon

Under a moon with a cheeky grin,
Laughter echoes, let the games begin.
A raccoon dressed in a posh bow tie,
Stole a sandwich with a twinkly eye.

The shadows waltzed with playful glee,
While frogs croaked beats to a symphony.
A starry fish jumped, reached for the sky,
Declaring itself the next big fry.

Crickets held a talent show, oh dear,
While owls served drinks, quite sincere.
With every hoot, a dance took flight,
Beneath the moon's glow, what a sight!

So follow the laughter, take a chance,
Join in the fun, and lose your pants.
For in the shadows, mischief thrives,
Where even the starlight humorously jives.

The Veil of Misty Horizons

On misty mornings, where the fog does play,
A clam wore a hat, in a quirky display.
With each wave's splash, it giggled and sighed,
While squids painted pictures, utterly fried.

The dolphins donned capes, ready for flight,
As seaweed danced in the soft, fading light.
A jellyfish tried to join in the fun,
But got tangled up—poor little one!

Seagulls debated who'd fly the best,
While snails took a selfie, feeling blessed.
With shells as frames, their portraits are grand,
Who knew that humor ruled this land?

So venture where horizons gently blur,
And find the joy that makes hearts stir.
With laughter mixing in the salty air,
It's the land of whimsy, beyond compare.

Echoes of Ancient Journeys

A treasure map, scribbled with a clown,
Leads to a spot where laughter's renown.
Pirate ghosts, with pirate pets,
Played charades, with no regrets.

Old ships tell tales of silly schemes,
Where sea turtles raced in dreams.
The compass spun, lost in delight,
As lobsters broke out in a dance at night.

Port holes peeked at a goofy cast,
With fishy jokes that would forever last.
A parrot squawked, "Adventure's the key!"
Join the club, let laughter be free!

So if you wander where echoes remain,
Expect surprises—joy's the gain.
For every journey holds a surprise,
With echoes of fun beneath sunny skies.

Where the Water Meets the Sky

The fish wear hats on sunny days,
And dolphins throw their flashy rays.
Seagulls gossip as they dive,
Telling tales of how they thrive.

Crabs with crutches walk the line,
While octopuses sip on brine.
A mermaid lost her golden comb,
Screamed, 'I've turned into a foam!'

Shells have debates on ocean trends,
While jellyfish play with silly bends.
A turtle's dance, though limited,
Is the highlight of the sunlit bit.

Waves clap hands in rhythm divine,
As boats juggle, sealing their shine.
With every splash and cheeky wink,
Nature prompts us all to think!

Mythic Creatures of Forgotten Depths

Mermaids fry up fishy fries,
While krakens roll their lopsided eyes.
Beware the shrimp with disco lights,
They dance till dawn in wild delights!

That sea horse thinks he's quite the star,
Racing submarines, oh how bizarre!
Nudibranchs don their rainbow gowns,
While anglerfish wear silly crowns.

A whale sings opera with a twist,
Leaving fish in a splashy mist.
Clams compete in beauty contests,
Pearls on stage, they honestly jest!

And bubbles float with laughter bright,
Telling jokes with all their might.
In waters deep where humor breeds,
Creatures live out their quirky deeds.

Shimmering Reflections of Lost Souls

Ghosts of sailors float and giggle,
While mermaids tease with a little wiggle.
Their echoes laugh through tides of blue,
Making waves that bounce and skew.

A pirate's parrot, lost in flight,
Spends the day in a feathered fright.
He tells tales of treasure and dread,
While a clam offers a cozy bed.

The fish wear shades, sunbathing bright,
While skeletons dance in pure delight.
Their shadows waltz beneath the moon,
Creating chaos, a watery tune!

In reflections where reality blurs,
The sea holds secrets, laughs, and purrs.
A graveyard of laughs floats near and far,
Where even lost souls wear a star!

Enigmatic Sandcastles in the Breeze

Sandcastles build with comedic flair,
Gates that tumble with no care.
A moat of jellybeans surrounds,
While gummy fish swim in bounds.

A crab dressed up as a royal king,
Waves his claws, demanding bling.
Seashells giggle, plotting their gotchas,
As seagulls swoop down, stealing nachas.

The tide brings snacks of seaweed chips,
While surfers practice flips and slips.
The sun bakes the sand into bliss,
A beach party, you don't want to miss!

As the evening draws curtains low,
A dance of shadows puts on a show.
With castles crumbling, still they gleam,
In this silly place known as a dream!

Mariner's Whispered Legends

Upon the waves, the stories sail,
Where fish wear hats and seagulls quail.
A pirate's parrot may just regale,
Of treasures lost in a mug of ale.

The octopus plays some tunes off key,
While crabs dance wildly, oh what a spree!
A mermaid chuckles, can't quite believe,
She's the life of the party, pure jubilee!

With every splash, a tale starts fresh,
Of sailors' blunders and fishy mesh.
Laughter echoes through the salty air,
As dolphins giggle without a care!

So raise your glass, to the sea's delight,
Where stories bubble in the moonlight.
For who knew waves could make us jest?
In humor's grip, we find our best!

The Ghost of the Ocean's Edge

At twilight's close, a ghost dons a cape,
He's got a tall tale, but can't find a shape.
A wisp of a wink, but not quite a sight,
Stumbles through fog, oh what a fright!

He trips on a wave, and how we did laugh,
Can't even float on a simple staff!
With humor and gags, he haunts in style,
Making the barnacles crack a smile.

With jellyfish friends, he throws a bash,
They dance on the tides and clash in a splash.
The seashells giggle, they've heard it before,
A ghost's funny bone is never a bore!

Though restless he roams, on the ocean's brink,
He shares all the laughs, as we all wink.
Tonight we shall toast to this merry scamp,
A ghost at the edge, forever a lamp!

Untamed Beauty Beyond the Driftwood

A driftwood king with a crown of seashells,
Whispers of wisdom and questionable spells.
He claims to be wise, yet trips on the sand,
While starfish chuckle and lend him a hand.

The tide brings laughter, like tickles from fish,
In the kingdom of sand, they all grant a wish.
The sandpipers dance with their tiny little feet,
While hermit crabs scoot in a fast-paced retreat.

They gather at dusk for a prehistoric show,
Where barnacles stand, putting on quite a glow.
The waves tell jokes, each one's more grand,
As laughter breaks out on the desolate strand.

In the wild of the coast, where the laughs are a riot,
Adventure awaits, no chance to be shy it!
For beauty is found in the silliest scenes,
In the kingdom of driftwood, where laughter intervenes!

Secrets Carried by the Current

The current whispers secrets to the shore,
Of turtles who tango and crabs that snore.
It carries the giggles of waves on their quest,
Among seaweed dancers, they jest and jest.

Old fish gather 'round to swap a tall tale,
About beaches where jellybeans grow without fail.
Their scales shimmer bright with laughter and fun,
As they face the horizon, ready to run!

The conch shell debates with a fishing line,
Who catches the best jokes, oh what a design!
Every splash brings a chuckle, a quirky twist,
As sea stars twinkle and try not to miss.

So listen closely, to the current's song,
Where humor and secrets so often belong.
For the tides will reveal, in a way that's absurd,
That laughter is buried in every waved word!

Whispers of Tidal Dreams

Beneath the moon, a fish wore a hat,
He danced on the waves, how silly, how fat!
Seagulls squawked, 'Is that quite a sight?'
As crabs joined the party, oh what a night!

Jellyfish jelly, a sweet, gooey treat,
They wobbled and jiggled, not one could compete.
Starfish were laughing, flipping about,
While shells rolled their eyes, oh what a clout!

A turtle with glasses weighed down by his shell,
Said, "I'm on a quest, wish me luck, wish me well!"
His friends threw him snacks, a fine fishy feast,
As he winked and he waved, laughing loud at the least!

At dawn, the sun beamed, a pancake surprise,
The ocean revealed its silly, bright lies.
With laughter and joy, they swam through the foam,
In a world where they danced, forever at home.

Hidden Currents of Time

In waters so deep, a clock was found,
Ticking and tocking beneath the ground.
Fish in tuxedos, all dressed up fine,
Sipped on seaweed and danced in a line.

The octopus juggled with shells on each arm,
While mermaids giggled, charmed by his charm.
A wave whispered secrets, old tales of yore,
Of pirates who danced, and treasures galore.

Crabs in a band played clinky-clank songs,
While sea cucumbers joined in with their throngs.
A dolphin with sparkles led the parade,
As bubbles with giggles made quite the charade.

So under the surface, where time takes a spin,
Laughter and mischief were sure to begin.
With a wink and a splash, they all twirled around,
In currents where joy and fun could be found.

Where the Ocean Hides Its Treasures

A crab found a treasure chest, oh so neat,
Filled with odd trinkets, a real tasty treat.
He opened it wide, expecting gold bright,
But in plopped a parrot, squawking with fright.

"Not exactly what I'd hoped to find here,
Wanna trade for a shell? Or maybe some beer?"
The crab scratched his claws, gave a blink, then laughed,
As the parrot just chuckled, "Well, I'm a fine craft!"

Seashells were scattered, pearls rolled and slipped,
While dolphins were busy, doing flips they equipped.
The treasure soon seemed more ridiculous than gold,
With hats made of seaweed and stories retold.

At last, with a grin, they all called it a day,
The ocean had hidden fun treasures to play.
With laughter and joy, they swam towards the light,
In a world where each find brought pure delight.

Beneath the Veil of Waves

A clam shared a joke that sent all fish reeling,
"Why don't we ever get caught out there stealing?"
The answers came quickly, in bubbles and cheer,
As fish giggled wildly, their laughter sincere.

A sea otter splashed, doing flips with a ball,
Challenging sea turtles to join in the call.
They shouted and cheered as bubbles went high,
Silly contests erupted with joy in the sky.

A whale belted tunes that echoed afar,
While sea urchins bobbed, the stars of the bar!
"Sing louder!" they clamored, as waves danced along,
In a concert of fun that went on far too long.

As night came to play, the moon winked a gleam,
The ocean rejoiced in a whimsical dream.
With curiosity swirling and laughter so bright,
They all nestled close, under soft shimmers of light.

The Lost Lull of Molten Sunsets

In the twilight glow, a crab did dance,
Clumsily waving, it thought it had a chance.
While seagulls laughed from the nearby rock,
The crab just shrugged; it was quite the shock.

As waves crashed down like a toddler's laugh,
Fish in the sea crafted jokes on behalf.
A starfish pondered, with a crooked grin,
"Why did the seashell just wear a fin?"

On the horizon, the sun took a dip,
The jellyfish giggled, it couldn't quite flip.
With a bubble burst, they all took a bow,
"Let's do it again—how do we get out now?"

As night fell down, they wore starry hats,
Pulled from their homes—those curious cats.
Laughter rang out, from water to shore,
In the twilight's clutch, they found room for more.

Solitary Footsteps Where Few Have Trod

A penguin waddled, alone with a grin,
Wondering just where all the fishes had been.
With a catchy tune, it slid on the ice,
Singing to seals, who thought it was nice.

Footprints behind him told tales of his ways,
Each one a story of clumsy delays.
A seal whispered loudly, "You're quite the odd chap,
But come join our party, it's all quite a snap!"

Down by the cove, he found fellow fools,
Crafting seaweed crowns in their make-shift schools.
Each dive was a splash, each laugh echoed wide,
In this quirky parade, they took all in stride.

As daylight faded, the penguin lay down,
Under a sky of a peculiar crown.
From shore to the ocean, they partied till dawn,
Those solitary steps had led him to swan.

The Whispering Shell's Confession

A shell on the sand, it swirled with a tale,
Claimed to be pirate, but was she just frail?
With each little whisper, she shared secret dreams,
Of swimming with dolphins, or so it seems.

"I'm a treasure!" she said, "Just wait for your chance,
I've got stories of sailors, oh come join my dance."
But nearby a clam heard the hullabaloo,
Said, "I don't believe you, I've seen quite a few!"

The sea foam giggled at the two on the beach,
"Tales of great danger, I'll let you both preach!"
Then crabs gathered round, their eyes wide with glee,
For the shell's tall tall tales were quite fun to see.

With laughter and jests filling the salty air,
They spun rounds of stories, both silly and rare.
In the glow of the dusk, they sealed it with glee,
As the shells whispered on, just shy of the sea.

Currents of Hope and Longing

A fish in a net, felt quite out of luck,
Dreaming of freedom but stuck like a duck.
With a wink to the waves, it began to declare,
"Let's play some tricks! There's fun in the air!"

With bubbles aplenty, a game soon took flight,
While dolphins joined in, what a splashy delight.
"Who can jump higher, or do the best flip?"
Laughter erupted, no sign of the trip.

A crab thought to join in, felt risk was the key,
But mistook the high dive for a simple spree.
Instead of a flip, it flipped right sideways,
The ocean erupted in cheerful displays.

When twilight arrived, they gathered in cheer,
With echoes of laughter that all could still hear.
On currents of joy, in the depths they did play,
A fish found its friends in the water ballet.

Crystalline Dreams at Dusk

At the beach, crabs dance with glee,
Wearing tiny hats, so fancy and free.
Seagulls gossip, making quite a fuss,
While surfers tumble, oh what a mess!

Waves whisper secrets with salty breath,
Jellyfish jelly is a taste of death.
Sandcastles crumbling, towers too tall,
As kids yell out, 'Look! I'm a wall!'

Lullabies of the Wandering Sea

The ocean hums a silly tune,
While floaties drift under the moon.
A fish wears glasses, can't see a thing,
As dolphins giggle and start to sing.

Turtles race, but never win,
With heads held high, they wear their skin.
Seashells chatter with tales quite grand,
Of mermaids dancing on golden sand.

Lost Treasures of the Depths

Old pirate hats are not quite right,
They float just like a kite in flight.
A treasure chest filled with socks and shoes,
Who knew pirates had such weird views?

Clams throw parties with shrimp and fries,
While fish make wishes, oh how time flies!
A treasure map marked with an 'X',
Turns out it's just a spot for tecks.

Enigma of the Quiet Shoreline

On the sand, a crab with a cane,
Says, 'I can't dance, but I can complain!'
Seashells gossip about old tall tales,
While starfish practice their ancient scales.

Footprints lead to a mystery plot,
Of a picnic gone wild—oh what a lot!
Kites tangled in seaweed, what a surprise,
As laughter echoes 'neath sunny skies.

When Secrets Linger in the Foam

Tiny crabs dance in a row,
Whispers of the tide's echo.
Seagulls squawk their secret tales,
While fish wear funny scales.

Waves giggle, tickling toes,
As beachcombers strike silly poses.
Drifting treasures in the sand,
Like odd socks, never planned.

Between the seaweed and the shells,
Silly stories have their spells.
A starfish waves its five small hands,
As laughter bubbles from the strands.

Sunsets paint the world with cheer,
Crabs' little jokes we long to hear.
So come and play upon the beach,
Where secrets linger out of reach.

The Last Message in a Bottle

A bottle floats, what could it say?
Maybe, "Help, I've lost my way!"
Or perhaps, "I need more cheese!"
Signed with an 'X', written with ease.

Beachcombers line up, all aglow,
Hoping to see the surprise below.
But mostly, they find old candy wrappers,
And one distinct, old catnip snappers.

Messages lost in ocean's sway,
Driftwood dreams that float away.
The secrets writhed in waves so sly,
Will always keep us wondering why.

So cast your wish into the tide,
Hoping for laughter to coincide.
Raise a toast with ocean's plea,
For humor floats so blissfully.

Echoes of Forgotten Mariners

Old boats creak with stories bold,
Of sailors lost to winds so cold.
Rumors swirl with salty air,
Of mermaids that don't really care.

Ghostly figures haunt the deck,
Playing cards and sharing a speck.
Each plucky tale met with a grin,
Of once, when they lost their fishy bin.

Giant squids, the rumored jesters,
Trading fish for silly festers.
The sea may hide what's yet to come,
But laughter's sure to make us hum.

So raise a flag, for sailors gone,
With tales of fun that linger on.
In the waves, their chuckles play,
Whispers of the sailors drift away.

The Unseen Path of the Ocean's Veins

Beneath the waves, a dance unfolds,
Invisible paths where laughter molds.
Fish with helmets plot their course,
Finding treasure, their favorite source!

Octopuses juggling, oh what a sight,
Throwing shells in the deep twilight.
While turtles giggle at their own grace,
In a slow-motion, underwater race.

Coral castles with a twist of glee,
Hosting a ball for sea debris.
Bang of a drum from a clamshell band,
As ebbing tides clap on the sand.

So dive below for secrets bright,
Where laughter swells with delight.
In the depths of ocean's maze,
Funny paths lead in quirky ways.

Compass Points to Mysterious Isles

If treasure maps could dance and twirl,
I'd trade my compass for a shiny pearl.
Each point a joke, each isle a pun,
Where mermaids giggle and the seaweed's fun.

With every turn, the winds would tease,
"Arrr, matey!" they'd say, "just sail with ease!"
Maps are for pirates, or so they claim,
But I just want riches from seas of fame.

The islands shift like a playful cat,
Who knows where they're hiding, tip of my hat!
Parrots squawk riddles, they never get old,
As I hunt for the chest with trinkets of gold.

So come aboard, join this comical quest,
Where laughter is currency, we'll be the best!
For every wave hides a chuckle or two,
In this wacky treasure hunt that's just for you.

The Silent Embrace of the Ocean

The ocean whispers jokes to the shore,
Telling tales of sailors and underwater lore.
Fish giggle softly, splashing in glee,
While crabs tell stories, sipping their tea.

Tides roll in with a cheerful knock,
Inviting all barnacles for a rock.
Shells are like drums, the waves play a tune,
Echoing laughter beneath the bright moon.

Seagulls swoop low, cracking jokes on the breeze,
As dolphins dance with grace, aiming to please.
"Why did the fish blush?" they wink and align,
"Because it saw the ocean's bottom, divine!"

So come take a dip, let giggles arise,
In the ocean's embrace, where humor lies.
For every splash hides a funny refrain,
The sea's a comedian, never mundane.

Remnants of Sailors' Secrets

Old maps are torn, with wrinkles galore,
But hey, who needs them when fun's at the core?
Sailors wrote secrets, but they wrote them wrong,
Their 'X' marks the spot always felt like a song.

Barnacle encrusted, they left behind clues,
Like treasure chests filled with old, funky shoes!
What did they find? Just tales of their fate,
And fishy aromas that no one could bate.

Lighthouses giggle in their light-house laughter,
Echoing tales of comical disaster.
"Why'd the sailor bring a ladder on deck?"
"To reach for the stars, what the heck?"

So, here's to the remnants of sailors so bold,
With secrets and laughter in each tale retold.
Let's celebrate quirks from the past without fear,
For who needs perfection when fun is so near?

Lullabies of the Whispering Winds

The winds sing sweetly, with melodies grand,
Tickling the sails, caressing the sand.
"Why aren't pirates what they used to be?"
"They just didn't have enough 'sea'-curity!"

Whispers of breezes blow by with grace,
Tickling the whiskers of curious fish face.
Each gust a chuckle, each breeze a jest,
A lullaby soft, where all trot their best.

The waves join in with a splash and a giggle,
As boats sway and dance, and gulls start to wiggle.
"What's a ship's favorite instrument?" they say,
"A bass guitar, because it can play all day!"

So let's raise a toast to the laughter we find,
In lullabies sung by the winds intertwined.
For every breeze that nudges our sails,
Holds stories of joy, where humor prevails.

Hidden Reefs of the Heart

There's a place where the sand tickles toes,
And the crabs wear their shells like fancy clothes.
Seagulls shout jokes, their laughs in the air,
While fish throw parties, without a care.

The tide rolls in with a cheeky grin,
Splashing our sunscreen on my best friend's chin.
We build castles with moats that collapse in a flash,
While clams gossip like neighbors in a splash.

Oysters hide their pearls, thinking they're smart,
But their glints give away every shy heart.
The starfish are seen, twirling around,
With a dance so funny, it's echoing sound.

So here's to the laughter that bubbles and flows,
In a land where the seaweed's a wig that just grows.
We'll trade all our secrets, a laugh and a cheer,
For hidden delights that keep us near.

When the Waves Keep Their Counsel

The waves gather round like a gossiping crew,
Spilling their tales of the ocean so blue.
Each splash tells a secret, a story anew,
While dolphins play tag, and they wing it, too.

A crab in a tux claims he's ready to dance,
But the sea cucumber won't give him a chance.
They argue for hours, in this watery show,
While sea urchins giggle, 'We'll never know!'

The moon's on the scene, sliding in with a grin,
Winks at the waves and they tumble within.
Together they chuckle, what mischief they bring,
While I sit with my sandwich, and hear them all sing.

Here's to the whispers, the splashes, the glee,
When the waves gather round, so much fun, can't you see?
In a world where the sand meets the glittery tide,
The secrets spill over, let's take a wild ride!

A Journey Beyond the Breaking Tide

Setting sail on a wobbly boat,
With a parrot that swears he can't float.
He squawks about treasure, all shiny and bold,
While I search for snacks, as my courage unfolds.

The seaweed waves back, it's quite a sight,
As the fish laugh together at their morning delight.
A rogue little jellyfish, swift on the chase,
Shoots past like a rocket, it's just a race!

"Arrhh!" cried the captain, with a flair so grand,
But his compass points home; oh, the irony he planned!
And the gulls, they just circle with questionable snickers,
How can one lose their way, amid nature's flickers?

We sail under rainbows, while dodging the shocks,
Making friends with the barnacles clustered in flocks.
With a hearty laugh, we bid the waves goodbye,
Adventuring onward, beyond the sky!

Beneath the Gaze of the Lighthouse

The lighthouse stands tall, a beacon of cheer,
With a light that goes 'swish' through the salty sea air.
It watches the boats as they fumble and roam,
Laughing at fishermen claiming, "This is my home!"

A gull steals my sandwich, quite bold and quite brazen,
While the lighthouse winks like it just made a raisin.
"Don't feed the birds!" it shouts with a grin,
As seagulls converge on the feast that's within!

The sailors share tales, with much bravado,
Of tightrope walking on kelp, oh, what a show!
But just out of reach, there's a barrel of laughs,
Where mermaids exchange their best seaweed crafts.

So let's toast to the tales told beneath this great light,
To secrets of laughter that twinkle at night.
For the waves and the wind must always conspire,
To keep us grinning and lifting us higher.

Uncharted Waters of the Mind

In a boat made of cheese, I set sail for a dream,
My compass is broken, or so it would seem.
The seagulls are laughing, they know where to go,
While I'm singing sea shanties that sound a bit slow.

The fish wear top hats, they swim with great flair,
They wink and they twirl, as if they don't care.
I barter with seaweed for treasures untold,
But end up with barnacles—my fortune's on hold!

Navigating mazes of jelly and jam,
Each wave a tickle, oh what a grand slam!
My thoughts are like flotsam, they bounce to and fro,
In this wacky old yacht that I call my mind's show.

As dolphins do pirouettes, I join in their jest,
In waters of nonsense, I'm truly the best!
With giggles and splashes, I've found my true aim,
Adventuring wildly, I forget all the shame.

The Calm Before the Storm

The sun's smiling brightly, with a wink and a nod,
Yet clouds are plotting mischief, oh how they prod!
Seashells gossip softly, sharing all their spice,
While crabs throw a party, so wild and precise.

I sip on my coconut, eyeing the sky,
As thoughts of great chaos begin to float by.
A parrot squawks nonsense, so loud and so clear,
'The calm is just clever, it's packing with cheer!'

With a splash and a dash, the waves start to rise,
But I'm still there laughing, no fear in my eyes.
Each droplet's a dancer, swirling in glee,
Beneath all this madness is still a grand sea.

So bring on the tempest, I'm ready for fun,
With rain as my confetti, we'll dance till we're done!
For laughter's my anchor, the storm can't outscore,
What's funny in chaos is worth so much more!

Dolphin's Dance at the Break of Dawn

As dawn kisses waves, a show starts to play,
Dolphins in tuxedos, they're leading the way!
With flips and with flops, they twirl in the light,
Each splash is a giggle, oh what a delight!

The sun peeks through curtains of lavender mist,
And all sleepy sea creatures can't help but insist,
That this waltz of the dolphins is grander than gold,
As they dance 'round the reef, both silly and bold.

I join the procession, my fins made of dreams,
With laughter like bubbles, we're bursting at seams.
To the rhythm of laughter, our hearts start to race,
In this ocean of joy, we've all found our place.

So here I shall stay, with these jesters of sea,
Each day is a circus, oh joy, what a spree!
With dolphins as partners, we cheer and we play,
While the world spins in wonder, in this watery ballet.

Cradled by the Sea's Embrace

Rocked by waves gentle, I drift through a dream,
Where seaweed's a blanket, its comfort supreme.
The fish throw me confetti, they shout with great glee,
As crabs judge the party, they wave cheerfully!

A starfish plays bingo, his smile is a star,
While turtles do tango, I cheer from afar.
With mermaids as waiters, they serve up delights,
I'm feasting on humor beneath the moonlight.

A pelican sings, and his tune is so sweet,
The sand's my soft pillow, my dreams feel a treat.
In waters adorned with laughter and light,
Every splash is a giggle, every wave feels just right.

So as I recline in this cradling swell,
I'll laugh with the waves, in this funny seashell.
For joy is the treasure that washes ashore,
And with every tide, I just find even more!

The Language of Forgotten Marinas

In a harbor of knives, the seagulls debate,
They squawk like old sailors, but carry no weight.
Creating a ruckus to chase off the fish,
Meanwhile, the jellyfish are wishing for swish.

The barnacles gossip, they cling with delight,
"Do you see that fine yacht, it's fearfully bright?"
While the rusty old boat just chuckles and grins,
"Back in my day, we were kings of the fins!"

A crab in a tuxedo performs a grand dance,
While clamming fish roll their eyes at the chance.
But when a wave splashes, it's all in good fun,
And they laugh at the chaos, for no one can run.

With anchors and nets, the stories unfold,
Of pirate adventures and treasures untold.
So raise up your glass, toast the nautical lore,
In this harbor of humor, we'll celebrate more!

Twilight Conversations with the Deep

Once twilight arrives, the fishes begin,
To share all their secrets as night settles in.
"Oh, did you hear how the octopus cried?,"
"She lost seven hats when the tide turned the tide!"

The starfish submit to a wave's funny swipe,
"Remember last summer? We danced with a pipe!"
They wiggle and giggle, performing their tricks,
While the sneaky old eel gets tangled in sticks.

A sea turtle nods with a wise, wrinkled grin,
"Don't take life too seriously, just swim in a spin."
And dolphins jump high, with their playful flank,
Splashing all jokes in the moon's silver tank.

So gather 'round seashells, and listen, you'll find,
These fishy debates are one of a kind.
With laughter like bubbles rising from deep,
There's magic found only in twilight's sweet sweep.

The Murmurs of Shells and Sand

In the chorus of shells, a clam starts to sing,
"Don't you wish you could wear my bling-bling?"
But the sand rolls its eyes with a light-hearted scoff,
"It's too much hassle when you just wanna scoff!"

A curious starfish chimes in with a grin,
"If you think that's fancy, just look at my skin!"
While crabs with their pinchers are drafting a plan,
To start a new fashion, 'The Sand-Crab Clan.'

With bubbles of laughter, the ocean joins in,
As fish trade their tales of where they have been.
"Oh, last week I dined on some seaweed surprise,
Yet the taste was all salty and came with some flies!"

As laughter erupts like the surf on the shore,
The shells whisper secrets and beg for some more.
In this bubbly realm where the creatures expand,
The humor just flows like the grains of the sand.

Ocean's Lullaby of Lost Legends

Upon waves that are laughing, the mermaids convene,
To banter and tease with a fresh fish cuisine.
"Did you hear of the sailor who fancied a whale?,"
"Oh, that's just a tall tale, a nautical fail!"

With shells on their heads and tridents in hand,
They whirl through the currents, a humorous band.
"Remember that time we tried catching a breeze?,"
"We ended up stuck in a net, oh dear me!"

The sharks zoom on by with a thrill in their voice,
"Competition was tough; we didn't have a choice!"
But the dolphins just giggle, they dance in delight,
As the krakens declare it a glorious night.

So lullabies echo through depths of the sea,
Where humor and legends blend joyfully.
With fish tales and theorists, the laughter grows wide,
In a world wrapped in wonder, where silliness bides.

Serenade of Silent Shores

At dawn, the waves begin to sing,
With silly seagulls on the wing.
They dance and dip, oh what a sight,
Chasing crabs in morning light.

A crab wore shoes, oh what a pair,
He strutted like he just don't care.
With tiny shades upon his eyes,
He'd shimmy through the sand and sigh.

A jellyfish with quite the flair,
Wore a tutu, floating in the air.
The starfish laughed, 'Oh look at him,
Living life like he's on a whim!'

The ocean's laughter fills the day,
As barnacles come out to play.
In silly games, they splash and splurge,
In waves of joy, their antics surge.

Beneath the Cloak of Night

Underneath the moon's bright grin,
The crabs hold parties with a spin.
They play limbo, while the fish toast,
To the happy shellfish, we love the most!

A dolphin wore a sparkly hat,
And danced along with a bouncing cat.
The shadows laughed as they twirled,
Making mischief in the darkened world.

The octopus juggled pearls with ease,
While the starfish clapped, saying 'Oh please!'
With every splash and every cheer,
The ocean's joy was crystal clear.

When morning came, with a bright fast light,
The laughter faded, what a sight!
But every night, beneath the glow,
They'll party again, the stars will know.

The Forgotten Hearth by the Sea

Once a crab found a treasure map,
But instead of gold, it led to a trap.
He dug for hours, full of delight,
And uncovered nothing but a fish's bite.

A clam said, 'Don't you feel quite strange?
Buried treasures rarely change!'
The crab replied, with a wink,
'At least I've got this missing stink!'

A mermaid popped by, with a grin so wide,
'You found your heart and stubbed your pride!'
The crab then laughed, abandoning the quest,
For laughter and friendship were truly the best.

Now they gather by the sandy hill,
With silly stories, they all sit still.
In the warmth of the hearth, with joy aglow,
They sing about treasures that truly grow.

Hushed Secrets of the Deep Blue

In waters deep where bubbles rise,
A fish told tales with goofy sighs.
A turtle laughed, with shell so bold,
'You won't believe what I've been told!'

The seaweed swayed, with gossip swift,
Spreading the news, like a real-life gift.
'Have you heard of the octopus dance?
He spins and twirls—oh, what a chance!'

A clownfish blushed, when asked to join,
But his friends cheered, 'Just have some fun!'
With fins that giggle, and flippers that play,
They found their joy in the splashes today.

So under the waves, the laughter flows,
With secrets whispered in watery prose.
In the depths of joy, the ocean sways,
With funny tales that brighten the days.

Enigmatic Sands of Solitude

Upon the dunes where napping crabs,
Stack their shells to form a cab.
I ask them, 'Where's the party now?'
They wink and scuttle, 'No one knows how.'

Seagulls gossip, spreading their wings,
Complaining loudly about beach springs.
The sunburned tourists sip on their drinks,
While dolphins giggle, oh what fun it brings!

Turtles race in slow-motion style,
While beach balls bounce with quirky guile.
Sandcastles crumble with a collapse,
And waves clap back with salty laughs.

Footprints vanish like ginger ale,
As the tide sweeps in with a cheeky tail.
A crab dons sunglasses, it's quite a sight,
On this sandy shore, the mood feels right!

Echoes of Forgotten Tides

Whispers rise from ocean's lips,
Fish in tuxedos dance in flips.
Crabs take selfies with coastal flair,
While seagulls plot their airborne dare!

The tide rolls in with quirky tunes,
Collecting hats and old typhoon loons.
A starfish juggles, quite a feat,
As jellyfish float with jellybean feet.

Seashells hide in clever plots,
Beneath the foam and laughing knots.
Sandcastles giggle, 'We're not so grand,'
Waving to the waves as they re-land.

The sun throws smiles, big and bright,
While otters splash, what a silly sight!
Every grain has its own chuckle,
As this shoreline sparkles, nothing's a huddle!

The Unseen Horizon Beckons

Behind the waves, adventure waits,
With sea cucumbers wearing skates.
A ship made of shells sailed on by,
With captain crab and parrot, oh my!

Mermaids giggle at silly sights,
While starfish practice their dance fights.
An octopus writes with eight fine pens,
Stories of wobbly deep-sea friends.

Kids race kites, casting their nets,
While plucky pelicans place friendly bets.
Clouds toss popcorn onto the sea,
Sons of the wind laugh, 'Join us, whee!'

Cookies tumble from coastal stores,
And penguins stage "Ninja" galores.
The unseen beckons, but don't be shy,
This joy on the horizon will surely fly!

Shadows in the Saltwater Mist

In the mist where shadows play,
Sand crabs negotiate their pay.
Seashells hold whispers of the past,
While fish tell tales of how they splashed.

Mermaids in shades of silly hues,
Complain about their finned blues.
As dolphins tease with acrobatic flair,
Each giggle floats through the salty air.

Waves crash down with playful might,
Chasing gulls that take swift flight.
A hermit crab dons a tiny sock,
Making beachgoers giggle, oh what a shock!

Under the sun, shadows twist and weave,
With laughter dancing, we shall believe.
For in this misty, sandy land,
The fun is wild, and life is grand!

Dreaming Along the Windward Path

I strolled along the sandy stretch,
With flip-flops flapping, oh what a sketch!
Seagulls squawked, they stole my fries,
While I tried to outrun my own sighs.

The sun was blazing, my hair a mess,
Squinting at clouds, what a lovely stress!
Shells whispered secrets, a snarky joke,
I laughed at the waves as they rolled and poked.

Crabs joined in, doing a little dance,
I wondered if they'd noticed my pants!
With jellyfish friends swimming near my feet,
I slipped on a rock and landed on wheat!

At dusk, the laughter echoed wide,
As I shared my tales on the goofy tide.
With each silly step, the day grew old,
Dreaming of antics, oh, stories bold!

Lighthouses of Lost Hope

Standing tall, the lighthouse beams,
But all I see are my past dreams.
It flickered like my brain at night,
As I pondered breakfast, what a sight!

The foghorn honked, I gave a cheer,
Confused, I waved to a passing deer.
They say it guides the sailors right,
But I got lost in that silly light.

Fishermen grumbled as they cast away,
Catching seaweed that tried to play.
I snorted at gulls in a fashionable dress,
Strut your stuff, birdie, you look a mess!

With each slap of waves, the humor rolled,
Stories of blunders, all retold.
In the glow of the beacon, I sat alone,
Doodling a map to my funnier throne.

When the Sea Calls for Silence

The beach was calm, too chill for chatter,
I heard a clam said, "What's the matter?"
My brain took a dive, like fish for bait,
Caught in thought, I felt like fate.

A crab sidled up, gave me a wave,
He said, "Life's too short to be so grave."
With each breeze, I giggled at fate,
Strange conversations with crustaceans await.

I tried to listen to the ocean's chat,
But all I heard was, "Ain't that a splat?"
As gulls serenaded, oh what a sound,
Needless to say, normal is drowned!

So I embraced the silence of noise,
Among the shells and bizarre toys.
Each splash and crash, a laugh or cry,
In the sea's deep whispers, I learned to fly.

Between the Rocks and Waves

Rocks stood firm, all rugged and tough,
While the waves splashed, saying, "That's enough!"
I slipped on one, my dignity lost,
Wishing I'd brought snacks, what a cost!

Between the boulders, I found a shoe,
The owner's nowhere, what shall we do?
I made a throne from sand and stone,
Proclaiming my rule as the crab king's clone!

Frogs joined in, forming a choir,
Croaking tunes like a rubber band fire.
With each wobble and wobble, laughter reigned,
While I sorted who's lost and who's gained.

So here I laugh, where weird meets swell,
Between the rocks, I'll weave my spell.
With waves as my band, I'm now the star,
In this rocky kingdom, I've come so far!

Beneath the Shimmering Surface

Bubbles rise, fish start to prance,
A hermit crab joins in the dance.
Laughing waves, they tickle your toes,
While seagulls steal chips if you doze.

Flip-flops flying, what a wild sight,
Running from waves that are just too light!
A tangle of seaweed, a hilarious catch,
You think you're a mermaid? Oh, what a match!

Sunburned noses, all red as a clam,
Making sandcastles, oh, what a jam!
A crab in sunglasses, looking so cool,
Poking its hat on a tiny stool.

In giggles and splashes, we find our glee,
Dancing with dolphins, come join the spree!
With each little wave, a chuckle, a sigh,
This watery world makes laughter fly high.

Veiled Horizons

Waves whisper secrets, but no one can hear,
A pirate's parrot squawks, "Arrr, bring me beer!"
Sandcastles wobble, the tide gives a poke,
Watch out! Here comes that splashy old joke!

On the horizon, a ship made of cheese,
Where mermaids giggle and do as they please.
An octopus juggles, what a crazy sight,
With clams as his audience, under moonlight.

Lighthouse beams twinkle, like disco balls bright,
As starfish do the salsa, a true dance delight.
Fish in tuxedos, at the reef's grand ball,
Invite you to join them, just give it your all!

Beneath the vast sky, where the sun likes to play,
We laugh with the sea, until the end of day.
With every giggle, the waves pulse and sway,
On this silly journey, come dance and stay!

Sandy Footprints in Twilight

Footprints leading where? No one can tell,
Chasing a crab that ran like a spell.
The sand feels so warm, like a giant hug,
Until flops of wetness make you feel snug.

Balloons floating by, a beachy parade,
A seagull looks jealous, eat that? No way!
With sunscreen on eyes, you squint at your friend,
While he shoots for the waves and tries to pretend.

Twilight tunes hum from a distant ice cream van,
As flip-flops snap loudly, oh, yes, that's the plan!
A race for the cones, running wild with glee,
The ocean spills laughter, it's as sweet as can be!

But wait! What is this? A jellyfish float,
We laugh and we splash, with a squeaky boat.
As evening arrives, with stars up on cue,
This merry mischief will always ring true!

Echoes of an Enchanted Coast

Shells scatter laughter across golden sand,
While turtles play chess, can you understand?
A dolphin with shades shoots a wink from afar,
As jellyfish glide like a fancy sports car.

The breeze starts to giggle, the sun's up for fun,
As flip-flops squawk, "Let's play till we're done!"
Kites soaring high, like very bold dreams,
Woven with laughter, bursting at the seams.

Even the crabs seem to hold a chitchat,
As they scuttle by with a curious pat.
Underneath a starfish, what do we spy?
A treasure chest filled with giggles and pie!

This miraculous coast, where we skip and we twirl,
With giggles and wonders, let imaginations unfurl.
As twilight approaches, we'll dance in the light,
Echoes of joy, in this magical night.

Secrets Whispered by Sea Glass

A shard of green, a tale so sly,
Once held a drink, now just a lie.
It sparkles bright in the sand, it seems,
Whispering secrets of forgotten dreams.

Bottles washed up from a lost old ship,
With messages scribbled on paper so crypt.
Yet when we read, it's all a mistake,
Just a grocery list for a fish fry bake.

Mermaids giggle as they pass on by,
Trading fish tales and quicksilver lie.
In this realm where odd things unite,
We laugh with the sea; oh, what a sight!

So here's to the glass that tells us a tale,
Of picnic lunches and the occasional whale.
With treasures so silly, washed ashore,
The ocean's a jokester, forevermore.

Embracing the Unfamiliar Shore

I wandered wide on the sandy spread,
Met a crab that danced, or so it said.
With claws held high, he made quite the show,
I fumbled and tumbled, shouting, 'Go, buddy, go!'

A seagull squawked as it dove for a fry,
It missed and fluffed up, looked straight at the sky.
With wings all askew, it took off in flight,
Chasing its dinner in a comical plight.

The waves rolled in with a bubbly grin,
As I chased my hat that danced on the wind.
The shoreline's my stage, where laughter ensues,
With antics from crabs and some silly old moose.

So I'll frolic and tumble on this strange land,
Where each little creature has a giggle planned.
Embracing the quirks, oh what a fun score,
On this jolly, wild, unfamiliar shore!

Merman's Lament Under Starlit Skies

Oh, woe to me, a merman so bold,
With scales that shimmer but tales that are old.
I lost my comb in the coral reef,
Now my hair's a tangle—what a comic grief!

Under starlit skies, I sing my plight,
A fish tried to dance, which gave me a fright.
With a flick of its tail, it missed my poor shoe,
Now I'm here barefoot, with a seaweed stew.

The jellyfish jiggle, they dance with glee,
While I'm stuck grumbling, 'Don't jiggle on me!'
Oh, for a quick rinse and a shampoo parade,
In the depths of the ocean, where mischief is made.

So hear my lament, ye creatures of the sea,
For a merman's life is not easy, you see.
Each star up above, a flicker, a wink,
In this watery world, I just need a drink!

The Last Tide of Sundown

The tide pulls back, whispering goodbyes,
As beach chairs tumble beneath the skies.
With umbrellas flapping like birds out of luck,
I chase my flip flop, oh please, don't get stuck!

The crabs are retreating, their claws all a-twitch,
As I make a mad dash, what a silly glitch.
Kids squealing loud while their sandcastles fall,
The ocean's a thief, can't we just have it all?

The seagulls are laughing, their jokes in the air,
About the last tide and my sad sunburned hair.
As stars start to peek from their velvet cocoon,
The ocean just chuckles, "See you soon!"

So I wave goodbye to the foolish, the fun,
As the sun dips low, day finally done.
In this final tide of a day to adore,
Life's a beach parody, who could ask for more?

Where Shadows Play in the Sand

Footprints dancing in a line,
Seagulls laughing, feeling fine.
A crab wearing shoes, what a sight!
Chasing the waves under sunlight.

Buckets abandoned, lost at sea,
A mermaid fussing with her tea.
Sandy napkins and shells to share,
Sandcastles built with utmost care.

But wait! A wave comes rushing through,
That castle crumbled, boo hoo hoo!
Laughter echoes all around,
As we splash and tumble down.

With shells and giggles in our bags,
Chasing shadows, oh how it drags!
At the end, we brush off sand,
Leave the beach hand in hand.

Forgotten Coves of the Heart

Tucked away where treasures hide,
Laughter echoes with the tide.
A rubber duck floats all alone,
In a cove that's barely known.

Seashells whisper, secrets bold,
While seaweed pranks, it's a sight to behold.
A crab recites a joke or two,
While we laugh and search for clues.

An octopus sketches on the sand,
Draws silly faces, isn't it grand?
With jellyfish bouncing like confetti,
Our worries vanish, feeling ready.

As the sun dips low in the glow,
We gather shells in a row.
Forgotten moments, what a start,
In silenced coves, we mend our heart.

Moonlit Secrets beneath the Waves

Under moonlight, fish parade,
Dancing shadows, a grand charade.
A starfish juggling by the shore,
While we laugh and always want more.

The tides reveal a hidden street,
With mermaids pouring drinks, oh what a treat!
A flounder slips while delivering a jest,
While everyone laughs, we're feeling blessed.

Clams recite poems with a twist,
Each line making us laugh as we insist.
They squirt water, a playful tease,
Enchanting nights like a gentle breeze.

So dance with waves, join the fun,
Laughing with critters till the night is done.
Beneath the moon, a party spree,
With fishy friends, we're wild and free.

The Untold Story of the Breeze

A breeze whispers jokes in the night,
Tickling cheeks with pure delight.
It carries laughter over the bay,
Where crabs and gulls join in the play.

Sand dunes giggle, shifting with flair,
As the ocean sings a song so rare.
"Why did the shell stay home all day?"
"Too much nonsense out here, I must say!"

Sailboats waltz with a clumsy grace,
While the wind bursts forth in a playful race.
The breeze, our comrade, never grows old,
Tells goofy tales, as laughter unfolds.

It flirts with the palm trees, sways them wrong,
Encourages us to join in the song.
The secret behind each gust that blows,
Is just us laughing where nobody knows.

Tales of the Enchanted Peninsula

Underneath the palm trees' sway,
A crab tried to dance, but slipped away.
Seagulls laughed at his silly prance,
The sun just chuckled, a bright romance.

A turtle wore sunglasses, thought he was cool,
While fish played poker using a shell as a tool.
The ocean giggled, its waves full of cheer,
As they splashed on the rocks, bringing humor near.

A mermaid came by, telling a joke,
But it fell flat, as the seaweed spoke.
She swam with a grin, her tail all a-swish,
Then swam right past, winking at a fish.

At twilight, they gathered for laughter and fun,
The sunset was clapping, a round of applause begun.
In the heart of the waves, where the antics abound,
Joy echoes forever, in magic they found.

Odes to Solitude in Salty Realms.

A clam sat home, all tucked in tight,
Dreaming of parties that last through the night.
An octopus dressed up in a snazzy bow tie,
But who can he dance with? Just the tide passing by.

A lonely old whale wrote a postcard bright,
To friends in the sea: "Come help my plight!"
With bubbles as ink and a wink for flair,
He sent it off swiftly on a slick ocean air.

A conch got gossip, a juicy, bizarre
About a fish that claimed he was once a star.
They all held their breath, waiting for proof,
Yet found only seaweed and a sunken roof.

As night fell gently, stars flickered above,
The sea whispered sweet nothings, like stories of love.
Still solitude reigned, with laughter afloat,
In these salty realms, all dreams take a note.

Whispers of Distant Waves

Waves chuckled softly, telling tales anew,
Of a crab who thought he could pop a wheelie, too.
The fish rolled their eyes, fins flapping with glee,
As he crashed into sand, saying, "Was that me?"

An otter played fetch with a brightly green ball,
But it slipped from his grasp, making a splashing call.
The ocean splashed back, in playful reply,
Rolling laughter that echoed beneath the sky.

A dolphin juggled shells, not quite on its game,
One flew far off, and they all lost the aim.
With a flip and a dive, they did take a break,
And laughed till they cried, oh what fun they make!

As the dusk set in, with colors aglow,
The waves kept the secrets, shifting to and fro.
In this world of whimsy, where joy takes a dip,
The whispers continue on their crafty trip.

Hidden Tides of Memory

Among the rocks lay a treasure so neat,
An old flip-flop washed up, with not much to beat.
A hermit crab claimed it, as fanciest gear,
Now strutting the beach, spreading laughter so clear.

A fish rode a surfboard, oh what a sight,
But wiped out so hard, disappeared from the night.
With bubbles around, his friends burst in cheer,
"Don't quit your day job!" They all hollered near.

An octopus wrote poems, with ink flying far,
It tried to impress a romantic star.
But each verse turned silly, much like a child's play,
Only laughter remained, as they swam away.

In the glow of twilight, memories would shine,
Of silly adventures, and moments so fine.
These tides keep on turning, with secrets they store,
Of laughter and joy, leaving hearts wanting more.

Surreptitious Shores of Solitude

There once was a beach, no one could find,
Where seagulls wore hats, quite unrefined.
They sipped on some soda, with ice and a wedge,
And argued for hours 'bout the sand's true edge.

Turtles in tuxedos, they danced on the sand,
With crabs playing banjos, oh wasn't it grand!
They held a parade, all under the sun,
And invited the starfish, now wasn't that fun?

A walrus played poker with seagulls in shades,
While dolphins provided the music charades.
The waves laughed so hard, they splashed the whole scene,
With jellyfish giggles, a sight to be seen.

So if you should wander, with laughter in tow,
Beware of the beach where wild creatures glow.
For there in the shadows, they cheer and they roar,
At that whimsical, wondrous, unfindable shore.

The Siren's Hidden Song

In waters where mermaids don pink, floral hats,
Their voices could lure even the best of the spats.
But instead of a wail, it's a tune made of fries,
And sailors, bewildered, decide it's all lies.

They croon about burgers and fizzy pop dreams,
Laughing as dolphins add in silly themes.
With seagulls on maracas and otters on drums,
Their band does a shuffle, oh my, here it comes!

Each sailor now dances, just caught in the beat,
While sand crabs play trumpet right down by their feet.
But oh, as they wiggle and jiggle around,
They trip on a seaweed, face-first in the ground.

The laughter erupts with each splash of the spray,
As mermaids throw seashells, come join in the play!
So heed this dear warning, if ever you roam,
The song of these sirens might feel like your home.

Reflections in the Tidal Pool

In a puddle of water, where stories unfold,
The fish share their secrets, if only you're bold.
They gossip of crabs and their fashionable shoes,
While snails slowly plot the next great ocean cruise.

A starfish named Larry, with a glimmering grin,
Told tales of the time he danced on a fin.
With bubbles for laughter and seaweed for flair,
They gathered to giggle and comb through their hair.

Anemones twirled in a swirling ballet,
While sea cucumbers hummed soft tunes of cliché.
The pool rippled gently, a seat for the show,
Where everyone's antics would steal the whole glow.

So if you find splashes that sink your own boat,
Just peek in the pool, it'll tickle your throat.
For every reflection holds laughter, my friend,
And sea critters plotting their antics won't end.

Glistening Coves of Longing

In coves where the sunbeams chuckle and play,
The merfolk play cards in a humorous way.
With octopuses dealing with eight-handed flair,
They giggle and snicker, no worries or care.

Clams snap to the beat of a jazzy sea tune,
While minnows create a conga line swoon.
They melt into laughter, but oh, what a plight,
For crabs start a wave that spills over, what a sight!

A flounder in sunglasses sips soup made of brine,
Pondering life in the bubbles of wine.
As whales sing a chorus, they keep it quite light,
Each wave brings a chuckle, each splash feels just right.

So off to those coves, if silliness calls,
You'll find laughter echoing through oceanic halls.
For in every nook, there's a giggle-extreme,
Along with a treasure chest filled with ice cream!

www.ingramcontent.com/pod-product-compliance
Lightning Source LLC
Chambersburg PA
CBHW072116070526
44585CB00016B/1475